Matt *and his*
Crazy Writing Machine

A Full-Length Play

by Lisa Soland

An All Original Play Publishing
Acting Edition

MATT AND HIS CRAZY WRITING MACHINE
Written by Lisa Soland
Copyright © 2008 by Lisa Soland

Published in 2024 by All Original Play Publishing
P.O. Box 32381
Knoxville, TN 37930
AllOriginalPlays@gmail.com

First Edition: March 2024
Printed in the United States of America
Graphic Design by All Original Play Publishing

ISBN: 978-1-956218-33-6
Library of Congress Control Number: 2024904197

What they're saying about...
Matt and His Crazy Writing Machine

"*Matt and His Crazy Writing Machine* is terrific!
Soland cleverly weaves the Sermon on the Mount
through the play in a way that will delight those
familiar with it. Those who are not will be
introduced to a charming canonical story made
all the more accessible by Lisa Soland's comical
style. *Matt and His Crazy Writing Machine*
presents a message we could all stand to hear for
the first or umpteenth time, whether in secular
or nonsecular venues."
– *Associate Teaching Professor, University of North
Dakota, Kathleen Coudle King*

"Soland has an amazing sense of humor and
knows her audience well. The characters sparkle,
the dialogue glitters, and like a diamond, it's a
jewel of a play."
– *Passionate Internet Voice Talk Radio Producer, First
woman-owned and operated Internet talk radio station,
Lillian Caldwell*

HISTORY

Matt and His Crazy Writing Machine received its world premiere at Theatre Encino in Los Angeles, California, on International Women's Day, March 8, 2008. It was directed by Lisa Soland, and Vincent Archer was the assistant director/stage manager. The cast, in order of appearance, was Todd Covert as *Matt*, CB Spencer as *Sarah*, David Purdham as *George*, Michael Blain-Rozgay as *Jesus*, Karesa McElheny as *Anna*, Scott Ford as *Saul*, Lee H. Page as *Echo*, and Paul McDade as *Luke*.

The comedy was the recipient of The International Centre of Women Playwrights Grant and was produced to help raise awareness and funds for homeless women in the San Fernando Valley through LSS and The International Centre of Women Playwrights.

Matt and His Crazy Writing Machine was then recorded live on the Internet on March 9, 2008, for Passionate Internet Voice Talk Radio (PIVTR). The broadcast was directed by Lisa Soland and produced by Lillian Cauldwell, with Joe Finera playing the role of Luke.

DESCRIPTION

Matthew has invented a writing apparatus he hopes will help him write as fast as Jesus speaks. The pen will make its debut on the day his rabbi delivers the most influential, life-changing speech of all time. But the distractions from the crowd are endless. Can this dedicated disciple capture the wisdom for the ages? We will see in this family-friendly, full-length comedy written by international playwright Lisa Soland.

This is a full-length, family-friendly play produced without intermission. It requires six males and two females.

6 m, 2 f

TIME: 30 A.D.

PLACE: A gently sloping hillside at the
             northwest corner of the Sea of Galilee,
             not far from Capernaum, on a
             beautiful afternoon.

CAST of CHARACTERS

Matt: One of Jesus' twelve disciples. An ex-tax collector and inventor of this new-fangled writing apparatus. He is a documentarian of sorts.

Sarah: A very attractive young woman. One of many who have climbed up the mountain to listen to Jesus.

George: An old, blind man. Kind and humble.

Jesus: The Son of God. Patient and kind beyond human comprehension. He is focused only on his Father, who is in heaven, and spreading the good news that we are loved, whether we deserve it or not, and we don't.

Anna: A deaf, older woman who is loud and occasionally obnoxious.

Saul: Sarcastic and charming, with a humorous personality. But ultimately, his heart is closed, and he is not open to believing much of anything about the Son of God.

Echo: A young man worried constantly about money and his day-to-day survival. He is currently working as an Echo—one who is hired by leaders of the day, like Caesar, to shout what is being said to others who are beyond earshot.

Luke: The only other gospel writer besides Matt to document the events of The Sermon on the Mountainside. He is more linear in his approach, and Matt thinks him less thorough.

Matt & His Crazy Writing Machine

SETTING: *A gently sloping hillside at the northwest corner of the Sea of Galilee, not far from Capernaum, in the year 30 A.D.*

AT RISE: *It is the afternoon, and MATT is busy organizing his papers and scrolls for what seems to be an important occasion. A very attractive woman, SARAH, is sitting nearby watching him. MATT begins to pour a black, liquid substance into what looks to be a hollowed-out twig.*

SARAH: *(Scooting close to MATT)* Excuse me?
    (Just as SARAH leans in, MATT flicks the side of the twig to make the liquid fall deeper into the twig, but a bit of the black substance hits SARAH in the face and tunic.)
MATT: Oh, I'm so sorry. I didn't mean to do that at all.
SARAH: Well, I shouldn't have leaned in like that. You didn't see me.
MATT: I didn't see you. Yes, that's right. *(Beat.)* Here, let me...
    (MATT takes out a handkerchief and dabs SARAH'S face.)
    There we go.

SARAH: Thank you. That's very kind.

MATT: Oh! There's some on your tunic, too. Here...

(He goes to quickly wipe that off as well but stops when he realizes that the blotch is on her chest.)

Excuse me.

SARAH: *(She looks down and sees what MATT was about to do.)*

Oh!

MATT: Here. Use this.

(MATT hands SARAH his handkerchief.)

SARAH: *(Dabbing the mark.)* Does it stain?

MATT: I don't know. I mixed it up this morning from some crushed grapes and ash.

SARAH: *(Nodding.)* Crushed grapes and ash.

MATT: Sorry.

SARAH: It doesn't sound very promising, does it?

MATT: Is that a new tunic or...?

SARAH: No, it's not new.

(Looks at MATT, reassuring.)

Honest.

MATT: Honest?

SARAH: I've had it a terribly long time.

MATT: *(Dismayed.)* So, you've grown attached to it, then.

SARAH: *(Handing him back his handkerchief.)*

Thank you for your handkerchief.

MATT: You can keep it. It's no good now. I'll never get that stain out.

SARAH: *(Smiling.)* All right.

(SARAH puts the handkerchief in her pocket.)

MATT: I wanted to come up with some sort of ink that wouldn't fade through time, you know? Something that would last the ages.

SARAH: I was going to ask; is that a twig you're holding?

MATT: Yes, it is. I hallowed it out so I could pour the liquid into this end, and then it would come out the point, down here.

SARAH: Does it work?

MATT: I sure hope so. I've been doing some test runs with it all morning.

SARAH: I use a feather. You don't like feathers?

MATT: They don't work fast. That's the problem. I need something that can write very fast so I don't have to keep stopping to dip. Write, dip. Write, dip. See? It slows you down. I need to be able to write as fast as someone speaks so I can document events as quickly as they happen.

SARAH: What's wrong with "*word of mouth*?"

MATT: I'm trying to eliminate misinterpretation.

SARAH: We've been using "*word of mouth*" for... Well, for as long as I can remember.

MATT: That's just it, don't you see? The information can only be passed on as long as *you can remember it*. And it can only be effectively passed on if you remember it *correctly*.

SARAH: I see.

MATT: What I'm documenting is far too important. There can be no room for error.

SARAH: What's this?

MATT: Oh, it's a book I'm working on.

SARAH: *(Reading.)* "The Sayings of Jesus." *(Beat.)*

You're one of them, aren't you?
(Motioning out beyond the audience.)
The twelve...uh...followers.

MATT: Disciples?

SARAH: Yes.

MATT: Well, we're *all* disciples, Miss—

SARAH: Sarah. You can call me Sarah.

MATT: Sarah. Yes, I'm one of the twelve.

SARAH: That's where I've seen you.

MATT: You've been to one of his sermons before?

SARAH: Why aren't you sitting up there with the others?

MATT: Luke's up there, and I can't sit next to him.

SARAH: Luke? Why?

MATT: It's disturbing. He thinks too linear.

SARAH: What do you mean?

GEORGE: *(Enters, then bumps into MATT.)* Excuse me.
    I didn't see you there.

MATT: *(To GEORGE.)* No problem.

SARAH: Are there 13 now?

MATT: Thirteen what?

SARAH: *(Trying to think of the right word.)* Uh...

MATT: Disciples?

SARAH: Yes.

MATT: No.

SARAH: Then who's Luke?

MATT: *(Frustrated.)* Oh, he's just running around
    interviewing everyone. Doing research. You
    know—a journalist, of all things.

SARAH: Oh, I see. *(Beat.)* And you're too good for a
    "journalist?"

4

MATT: It's not that. It's just his way of thinking. It messes with my head. Gets me all mixed up inside.

SARAH: You're going to have to give me an example.

MATT: Okay.

(He takes a breath.)

We're on a mountainside, right?

SARAH: Yes. I'd say so.

MATT: Luke will say we're on some kind of plane.

SARAH: Flat ground?

MATT: Yes, exactly! "Flat ground." In fact, he thinks flat. And his writing's flat, too. And the Word is so... poetic, really. Truth. Truth, by nature, is poetic because it rings true in our souls.

SARAH: *(Slightly embittered.)* I know about ringing poetry. Go on.

MATT: Well, I can't let Luke's version of things go down as the quintessential...sermon on the mountainside, can I? *(Beat.)* Ah! "Sermon on the Mountainside." *(Beat.)* That's good. I better write that down. I have to write things down right away, or I forget them.

SARAH: *(Reflecting.)* "Sermon on the flat ground." No, I think you're right. "Sermon on the Mountainside" has a much better ring to it.

MATT: After all, we are on a mountainside.

SARAH: *(Looking down behind her.)* That we are.

MATT: It's my job to be accurate.

SARAH: And poetic?

MATT: If it calls for poetry, as I have found truth can, I will be poetic.

SARAH: *(Bitterly.)* I was married to a poet once. *(Beat.)* It didn't work out.

MATT: I'm sorry to hear that.

SARAH: You're kind. *(Beat.)* I'll look forward to reading your book.

MATT: You won't have to read it. You're here. You are one of the blessed ones. You get to hear the message live for the first time—from the source!

SARAH: I suppose that is a blessing, isn't it?

MATT: We won't know how much. Not in our lifetime. But I've got a feeling.

GEORGE: *(To MATT.)* Excuse me?

SARAH: *(To MATT, seeing that he has others to talk with.)*
Thank you, uh—

MATT: Matthew.

SARAH: Matthew. Sorry to have taken up so much of your time.

MATT: No problem.
(SARAH crosses away and sits.)

GEORGE: Excuse me, but you seem to be in the loop. When is this thing going to start?

MATT: *(Looking forward beyond the audience.)*
Any minute now. He's praying, and he always prays right before he speaks.

GEORGE: Which one is he? Could you point me in the direction where he'll be standing?

MATT: He's the one with all the light around him. There.

GEORGE: What light?

MATT: Can't you see the light?

GEORGE: *(Shakes his head.)* No, I can't.

MATT: *(Sarcastically.)* If you can't see that light, you
must be blind.

GEORGE: Actually, I am.

MATT: Oh, sorry. It was just a figure of speech.

GEORGE: That's why I'm here. I thought maybe if he
had some time afterward... I mean... Well, a lot of
people must be here for the same reason, right?
To be healed.

MATT: The mountainside is crowded—like an ocean full
of lost sheep.

GEORGE: *(Sadly.)* The hunger of humanity.
(But with hope.)
But I've heard all he needs to do is touch you.

MATT: Sometimes, not even that.

GEORGE: It's hard to believe.

MATT: But it's true, nonetheless. I've been witness to
these things over and over again.

GEORGE: If it works, it can't take up too much of his
time, right?

MATT: You're going to have to have *some* faith.

GEORGE: I'm afraid I don't have too much of that left.
These are difficult times, and I've been blind
since birth.

MATT: He says if you have faith the size of a mustard
seed, you can move a mountain.

GEORGE: A mustard seed? Is that what he says?

MATT: Yes.
(Looks back at the pages in his journals.)
Let me get it exactly right for you. Here.
(Reads to GEORGE.)

"For truly I say to you, if you have the faith the size of a mustard seed, you will say to this mountain, 'Move from here to there,' and it will move, and nothing will be impossible to you."

GEORGE: Isn't that something? *(Beat.)* A mustard seed isn't very big at all, is it?

MATT: Nope. It's tiny. Here.

> *(MATT picks up a tiny pebble from the ground and places it in GEORGE'S hand.)*
> Feel that?

GEORGE: Yes.

MATT: That's all the faith you need.

GEORGE: I think I can "mustard" up that much. *(Beat.)* Get it? "mustard" up that much?

> *(THEY laugh.)*

MATT: *(Looking forward, with urgency.)*
> He's finishing up now. You better have a seat.

GEORGE: You've been kind. Thank you, young man. Do you mind if I sit here?

> *(He sits beside MATT.)*

MATT: Where's my apparatus?! I've misplaced my...

> *(Noticing it beneath GEORGE.)* You're sitting on it. Do you mind?

GEORGE: I thought I felt something...askew.

> *(Moving a bit.)*
> Sorry about that, young man.
> *(Hands MATT the tool.)*

MATT: No problem.

> *(Taking the twig of wood from GEORGE.)*
> It's something I put together so I can write down each word that's spoken.

GEORGE: Documenting the event, are you?

MATT: I'm going to try.

GEORGE: All you can do is your best, young man. That's all you can do.

MATT: Yes, but getting things right is hard.

GEORGE: Life's hard.

MATT: *(Referring to the other disciples sitting out front.)*
The other disciples? They all have memories like elephants, but me?! I've got to write it all down, or it goes right out of my head. *And* I've got to get it word perfect. After all, he is the long-awaited—

JESUS: *(From offstage, behind the audience, unseen.)*
Blessed are the poor in spirit, for theirs is the kingdom of heaven.

MATT: Here we go. Off and running.
(MATT begins to write.)

JESUS: Blessed are those who mourn, for they shall be comforted. Blessed are the meek, for they shall inherit the earth.

MATT: *(Writing away.)* Amazing. He always starts out with the most powerful stuff. Blows my mind.

JESUS: Blessed are those who hunger and thirst for righteousness, for they shall be satisfied.

MATT: *(Writing.)* "...hunger and thirst..."
(To SARAH, who is within earshot.)
See what I mean? Poetic. This stuff is pure poetry.

SARAH: *(With bitterness.)* It's poetry, all right. But it is beautiful.

GEORGE: *(With complete peace on his face.)* It most certainly is.

JESUS: Blessed are the merciful, for they shall obtain mercy.

MATT: *(Writing fast.)* "...merciful...mercy..."

JESUS: Blessed are the pure in heart, for they shall see God.

GEORGE: "They shall *see* him." Is that what he said? They shall "see"?

MATT: Yes, but he's talking about seeing with our perception of faith—

JESUS: Blessed are the peacemakers, for they shall be called sons of God.

MATT: He's saying you'll be able to see him one day— in the glory of heaven.

GEORGE: But I want to see him *now*.

JESUS: Blessed are those who are persecuted for righteousness' sake, for theirs is the kingdom of heaven.

MATT: *(Looking at his own arm.)* Ah! There they are!

GEORGE: Who? Who's there?

MATT: Goosebumps.

GEORGE: Who's he?

MATT: No, goosebumps. On my skin. See?
(MATT takes GEORGE'S hand and places it on his arm.)

GEORGE: Oh, why sure.

MATT: He always gives me goosebumps. That's how I knew.

GEORGE: Knew what?

MATT: Knew that I was to follow him. When he asked me, I got goosebumps.

JESUS: Blessed are you when men revile you and persecute you and utter all kinds of evil against you falsely on my account. Rejoice and be glad, for your reward is great in heaven.

MATT: Persecution carries with it God's blessing. We can be grateful for that.

GEORGE: But that doesn't make it any easier.

(ANNA enters and sits upstage of MATT.)

MATT: *(Looks up.)* He's pausing. He always pauses between subjects. He must be done with that section.

(Stands and paces due to the excitement.)

Let's see: 1, 2, 3, 4, 5, 6, 7, 8, 9. It must lead somewhere—nine. Let's see. The order must be relevant. It's all relevant. You have to know that going in.

ANNA: *(To MATT.)* Excuse me, could you please sit down? Your head is very big, and it's in my way.

MATT: Oh, sorry. *(MATT sits, then whispers to GEORGE.)*

Is my head big?

GEORGE: Bring it here.

(MATT leans in, and GEORGE feels MATT'S head with his hands.)

It's no mustard seed.

MATT: Never mind.

(To self, picking up his papers.)

Let's see what we have here. It's basically the Ten Commandments but updated and more tangible.

(MATT takes a sip of water from his leather water skin.)

GEORGE: So, you say he came to you and asked you to follow him?

MATT: I was working my booth beside the road, by the shore of the Sea of Galilee. He had just recruited Andrew and Simon, who were fishing down there, and they were headed—

JESUS: *(Beginning again.)* You are the salt of the earth...

MATT: Oh, excuse me.

(Returns to writing.)

GEORGE: Writing?

MATT: Yes.

GEORGE: *(Encouragingly.)* Good for you! Don't let me interrupt.

JESUS: *(Continuing.)* But if salt has lost its taste, how shall its saltness be restored?

ANNA: What? What did he say?

MATT: *(Writing frantically, then to himself.)* "...how shall its saltness..."

ANNA: *(Scooting to sit closer to MATT.)* Excuse me. You're writing all this down, aren't you? Could you please repeat that last line? I didn't get it.

MATT: *(Sarcastically.)* Let me guess. You're deaf, right?

ANNA: What?

MATT: *(Louder.)* Deaf?!

(Realizing she is. To self.)

Dear me.

ANNA: I know it's about God, but what specifically did he say just a moment ago?

MATT: *(Trying to be patient, he quickly looks at notes.)* Let's see...

(Finding the last line spoken, he reads it to ANNA.)

"If salt has lost its taste..."

ANNA: Yes?

MATT: "...how shall its saltness be restored?"

ANNA: That's a good question, but why are you asking me? I've come to learn, not teach.

JESUS: You are the light of the world. A city set on a hill cannot be hid.

MATT: *(Writing.)* "...hill..."

JESUS: Nor do men light a lamp and put it under a bushel, but on a stand, and it gives light to all in the house.

ANNA: *(To MATT, loudly.)* What? What did he say?

MATT: *(Losing patience, he suddenly rises and talks loudly to those sitting around him.)*

We need an Echo here. Please? Could someone please stand in as an Echo for this woman? Ours didn't show up today.

(MATT waits, then gives up and sits frustrated.)

Well, I tried.

ANNA: *(Whispering to MATT.)*

Why did you do that? We were doing fine.

MATT: *(To ANNA.)* I'm writing here—

JESUS: Let your light so shine before men...

MATT: I need to write. *(To GEORGE.)* What did he just
     say? I missed it.

ANNA: *(To MATT.)* If you need to write, WRITE. I'm
     not stopping you.

JESUS: ...that they may see your good works.

GEORGE: *(To MATT.)* "Let your light so shine before
     men..."

JESUS: ...and give glory to your Father who is in heaven.

GEORGE: "...that they may see your good works...and
     give glory to your Father who is in heaven."

MATT: *(Frantically finishes writing it.)* Great. Thanks
     so much. *(Looks at his pen.)* It's working.

ANNA: What?

MATT: My apparatus. It's working!

GEORGE: Good for you.

ANNA: I still can't hear him, especially with you two
     jabbering away! Jeez, whiz!

MATT: *(To ANNA.)* Move closer. Did you ever think of
     that? Moving closer?

ANNA: Only the ones who are *close* to him get to sit that
     close.

MATT: And now I know why they do.

SARAH: Actually, I can't hear him either. This whole
     section over here is experiencing some sort of
     low volume.

ANNA: Maybe it's the direction he's facing.

SARAH: Could be.

ANNA: Go up there and tell him to face us.

MATT: *(Rises and addresses the group.)*
     Listen, all of you. Quickly. He does nothing
     haphazardly. Okay? He led us up this

mountainside because the acoustics are good *here*, so if you could simply be quiet and *listen* and trust his non-haphazardness—

JESUS: *(Continuing.)* Think not that I have come to abolish the law and the prophets; I have come not to abolish them but to fulfill them.

GEORGE: *(Whispering to MATT so he can write and listen at the same time.)*
I could be her Echo if you'd like. I hear rather well.

MATT: *(Not hearing GEORGE.)* What?

GEORGE: Better than you, young man.

JESUS: For truly, I say to you...

MATT: *(Whispering to GEORGE while he writes.)*
Great. But do it quietly. Please.
(GEORGE moves close to ANNA and repeats everything JESUS says, to her, quietly, so we can barely hear him.)

JESUS: ...till heaven and earth pass away, not an iota, not a jot...

MATT: Not one meager stroke of the pen—

JESUS: ...will pass from the law until all is accomplished.

ANNA: *(To GEORGE.)* This is very kind of you.

SARAH: *(To GEORGE.)* For me, too, please. I'm having a hard time as well.

GEORGE: *(To SARAH.)* Sit close so I can keep my voice down.

SARAH: *(Scooting closer.)* How's this?

GEORGE: Closer.

SARAH: *(Scooting closer.)* This?

GEORGE: Lovely. Is that jasmine you're wearing?

SARAH: Why, yes.

MATT: Dear me. I thought you were blind!

GEORGE: Loveliness doesn't require eyesight.

JESUS: Whoever then relaxes one of the least of these commandments...

MATT: *(To self.)* Commandments! I thought so.

JESUS: ...and teaches men so, shall be called least in the kingdom of heaven, but he who does them and teaches them shall be called great in the kingdom of heaven.

MATT: *(Writing and talking to self.)* "Teaches them... shall be called great..."

JESUS: For I tell you, unless your righteousness is greater than that of the scribes and Pharisees, you will never enter the kingdom of heaven. *(Pause.)*

MATT: *"Greater than the Pharisees?!"* That's not possible.
(Finishes writing.)
Hey, you gotta love these pauses, huh?
(Looks around. Everything's fine.)
Great. Is everybody okay now?
(Next three lines are simultaneous.)

ANNA: Yes.

SARAH: We are. Thank you.

GEORGE: You just mind your writing there, young man.

MATT: Great.
(Takes a breath, relaxes.)

JESUS: You have heard that it was said to the men of old, 'You shall not kill, and whoever kills shall be liable to judgment.

MATT: There you go, "Thou shalt not kill." Sixth commandment.

JESUS: *(Continuing.)* But I say to you that everyone who is angry with his brother shall be liable to judgment...

MATT: Yikes.

GEORGE: Ouch.

JESUS: ...whoever insults his brother shall be liable to the council...

MATT: Double yikes.

GEORGE: Ouch, ouch.

JESUS: ...and whoever says 'You fool!' shall be liable to the hell of fire.

MATT: Triple yikes.

GEORGE: I got burned just listening to him say it! Does he really expect us to do this stuff?

MATT: *(Seriously.)* Yes, he does. But not by using our own power.

GEORGE: We need *him* to be able to do it.

MATT: Exactly.

JESUS: So, if you are offering your gift at the altar, and there remember that your brother has something against you, leave your gift there before the altar and go; first be reconciled to your brother, and then come and offer your gift.

MATT: He's moving beyond the Old Testament with this stuff.

JESUS: You have heard that it was said, 'You shall not commit adultery.' But I say to you that everyone who looks at a woman lustfully has already committed adultery with her in his heart.

MATT: *(Looks over at SARAH.)* Hi there.
(A little wave.)

SARAH: *(Looks back at MATT, then returns his little wave.)*
Hi there.

GEORGE: *(To MATT.)* It's a good thing I couldn't *see* when I was a teenager.

MATT: I hear ya.

JESUS: If your right eye causes you to sin, pluck it out and throw it away. It is better that you lose one of your members than that your whole body be thrown into hell.

GEORGE: Well, thank God for little miracles.

MATT: He means that we must deal drastically with sin.

GEORGE: Well, my eyes wouldn't be much of a loss for me.

JESUS: And if your right hand causes you to sin, cut it off and throw it away.

GEORGE: Now, that would hurt.

JESUS: It is better that you lose one of your members than that your whole body go into hell.

MATT: It's about ridding ourselves of the sin.

JESUS: It was also said, 'Whoever divorces his wife...

SARAH: Quiet, quiet.

JESUS: ...let him give her a certificate of divorce.' But I say to you that everyone who divorces his wife, except on the ground of chastity, makes her an

adulteress, and whoever marries a divorced
woman commits adultery.

SARAH: *(Sarcastically.)* Well, nothing like wrapping up
my body and sealing the tomb!

GEORGE: Are you divorced?

SARAH: Yeah. A poet. Never marry a poet.

(SAUL enters.)

JESUS: Again you have heard that it was said to the men
of old...

SAUL: *(He sits next to MATT and watches him write.)*
That's no feather.

*(MATT slowly turns to look at him, then
continues to write.)*

JESUS: You shall not swear falsely but shall perform to
the Lord what you have sworn. But I say to you...

MATT: *(To SAUL.)* Do you mind?

SAUL: Don't let me disturb you.

JESUS: Do not swear at all, either by heaven, for it is the
throne of God, or by earth, for it is his footstool,
or by Jerusalem, for it is the city of the great
King.

SAUL: Don't you love it when he does that?

MATT: *(Writing.)* Does what?

SAUL: Refers to himself in third person.

(Mocking JESUS.)

"Jerusalem, the city of the great king." *(Beat.)* It's
almost like he was suggesting that he, *himself*,
was God.

JESUS: Let what you say be simply "Yes" or "No."
Anything more than this comes from evil.

MATT: *(Listening intently to JESUS, he is able to control his anger at SAUL.)*
"Yes."

JESUS: You have heard that it was said, 'An eye for an eye and a tooth for a tooth.'

SAUL: What is that in your hand, there?

JESUS: But I say to you, do not resist one who is evil.

MATT: *(Listening to JESUS and then trying to do what he says.)*
"Yes."

SAUL: Yes, in your hand there?

JESUS: But if anyone strikes you on the right cheek, turn to him the other also.

MATT: My writing apparatus.

SAUL: That's no feather!

JESUS: And if anyone would sue you and take your coat, let him have your cloak as well...

MATT: Yes, that is correct. It is not a feather.

SAUL: Can I see it?

MATT: I'm using it.

JESUS: If anyone forces you to go one mile, go with him two. Give to him who begs from you, and do not refuse him who would borrow from you.

SAUL: *(Looks up to JESUS.)* Oh, you listen...but you don't listen well.

MATT: When I'm done, I would be happy to let you *look* at it.

SAUL: I can wait.
(With poignancy.)
I've become very good at waiting.

JESUS: You have heard that it was said, 'You shall love your neighbor and hate your enemy.' But I say to you, Love your enemies and pray for those who persecute you...

MATT: Uhm... "Love your enemies."

JESUS: ...so that you may be sons of your Father who is in heaven; for he makes his sun rise on the evil and on the good, and sends rain on the just and on the unjust. For if you love those who love you, what reward have you? Do not even the tax collectors do the same?

SAUL: How 'bout you, tax collector? Do you do the same, Levi? Only love those who love you?

MATT: *(Suddenly understanding.)* Oh, that's it. You knew me from before, and now you have come to torment me.

SAUL: Torment? *Me* torment?

JESUS: And if you salute only your brethren, what more are you doing than others? Do not even the Gentiles do the same? You, therefore, must be perfect, as your heavenly Father is perfect. *(Silence.)*

MATT: "Heavenly Father is perfect..." Done.
(Finishes writing, looks up to JESUS who has paused. He then hands the apparatus to SAUL.)
Okay, quick. Take a look.
(SAUL takes MATT'S writing apparatus from him and studies it.)

SAUL: I've not seen one like this. Where did you get it?

MATT: I didn't "get it." I made it.

SAUL: Make me one.

MATT: No.

SAUL: Why?

MATT: Honestly?

SAUL: *(Pointing front.)* You're one of them, aren't you?

MATT: Yes.

SAUL: I would expect nothing less.

MATT: *(Telling the truth.)* Because something doesn't feel right about making you one.

SAUL: Oh, well. Life stinks, and you don't always get what you want.

JESUS: *(Beginning again.)* Beware of practicing your piety before men in order to be seen by them, for then you will have no reward from your Father who is in heaven.

MATT: I'll have it back now. *(Holds out hand.)*

SAUL: *(Not giving it back.)* Are you listening, Matt?

MATT: My name is Matthew.

SAUL: So I've heard...*publican.*

JESUS: So, when you give alms, sound no trumpet before you...

SAUL: "Piety." He just said, "Beware of practicing your piety before men."

MATT: My apparatus, please?

JESUS: ...as the hypocrites do in the synagogues and in the streets, that they may be praised by men.

SAUL: *(Pulls dictionary out of pocket.)* "Piety." Let's see what my dictionary says. Ah, here it is. "Piety —devotion to religious duties."

MATT: I have a very important job to do here, which is why I invented this machine, so please. Can I—?

SAUL: *(Correcting him.)* "May I?"

MATT: ...have it back now?

SAUL: You are devoted. No one can deny that...Matt.

MATT: Matthew.

SAUL: I'll bet your devotion pleases him.

MATT: Please. I'm missing some valuable words.

> *(SAUL begins to sing a silly song, ignoring Matthew. He dances with the writing apparatus. MATT closes his eyes and takes a long breath. Remaining calm, he says nothing. He is listening and desperately trying to do and put to memory what is being said by JESUS.)*

JESUS: Truly, I say to you, they have received their reward. But when you give alms, do not let your left hand know what your right hand is doing.

SAUL: Left hand...

> *(Moving pen back and forth between hands.)*
> ...right hand. Left hand...right hand.

JESUS: So that your alms may be in secret, and your Father who sees in secret will reward you.

MATT: *(Quietly, with eyes closed, prayerfully.)* My heavenly Father will reward me.

SAUL: Ouch!

> *(Suddenly, SAUL is swatting at flies that seem to be biting him on the neck and buttocks.)*
> Ouch. These stupid, irritating, nettlesome bugs!
> *(While SAUL slaps, MATT'S apparatus falls to the ground.)*
> Where did they come from, anyway? Suddenly out of nowhere. Ouch.
> *(Slapping away.)*

You did this, didn't you?! You called these biting nemeses out of the woodwork to be rid of me! *(Slaps himself.)*
Well, we'll see about that.
(SAUL runs away.)

MATT: A lucky break for me.
(MATT picks up his writing apparatus, sits ready to write again, then looks into the heavens and whispers.)
Thank you.

JESUS: So when you pray, go into your room and shut the door and pray to your Father who is in secret, and your Father who sees in secret will reward you.

MATT: "Pray to your Father who is in secret..."

JESUS: And in praying, do not heap up empty phrases as the Gentiles do; for they think that they will be heard for their many words. Do not be like them, for your Father knows what you need before you ask him. Pray then like this—Our Father who art in heaven, Hallowed be thy name.
(Everyone on the mountainside recognizes that they are being taught something very, very important. Those who could not hear before, suddenly hear just fine. They begin to repeat after JESUS.)

EVERYONE: "Our Father who art in heaven, Hallowed be thy name."
(MATT continues to write as he prays along with the others.)

JESUS: Thy kingdom come...

24

EVERYONE: "Thy kingdom come—"

JESUS: Thy will be done, on earth as it is in heaven.

> *(They begin to cross downstage and form a line facing the audience.)*

EVERYONE: "Thy will be done, on earth as it is in heaven."

JESUS: Give us this day our daily bread...

EVERYONE: "Give us this day our daily bread."

JESUS: And forgive us our debts, as we also have forgiven our debtors.

> *(MATT has also become completely engaged in this spiritual moment. He sets aside his writing and crosses downstage.)*

EVERYONE: "And forgive us our debts, as we also have forgiven our debtors."

JESUS: And lead us not into temptation, but deliver us from evil.

EVERYONE: "And lead us not into temptation, but deliver us from evil."

JESUS: *(Straight through...)* For if you forgive men their trespasses, your heavenly Father also will forgive you; but if you do not forgive men their trespasses, neither will your Father forgive your trespasses.

MATT: *(To self.)* Forgive.

> *(Deep from his heart.)*

Father, please. Teach me how to forgive.

SAUL: *(Reenters with several band-aids covering his many wounds and carrying a variety of items. He looks at the line the others have formed.)* What is this? *A Chorus Line?*

(To MATT.)

Miss me?

(MATT turns away and, along with the others, returns to his original position.)

SAUL: I'm starved.

(He takes out his "sack lunch" and begins to chow down in front of Matthew.)

JESUS: And when you fast, do not look dismal like the hypocrites, for they disfigure their faces, that their fasting may be seen by men.

(SAUL is eating rigorously, and MATT begins to watch him hungrily.)

JESUS: *(Continuing.)* Truly, I say to you, they have received their reward. But when you fast, anoint your head and wash your face that your fasting may not be seen by men but by your Father who is in secret; and your Father who sees in secret will reward you.

SAUL: Matt, you look famished. You're not fasting, are you?

MATT: I'm fine.

(Attends to his writing.)

SAUL: Are you sure? I have plenty.

MATT: I can see that.

SAUL: I could share. I experience great rewards when I share.

MATT: No, thank you.

SAUL: Suit yourself, big guy.

(SAUL finishes the food and puts away leftovers. He pulls out a lawn chair, a small table,

Starbucks coffee, suntan lotion, and a hat to protect himself from the sun.)
But as for me, I choose to fully enjoy the blessings that the good Lord has graciously provided for me.

JESUS: Do not lay up for yourselves treasures on earth, where moth and rust consume and where thieves break in and steal, but lay up for yourselves treasures in heaven, where neither moth nor rust consumes and where thieves do not break in and steal. For where your treasure is, there will your heart be also.
(MATT looks at SAUL.)

SAUL: *(Offering him some.)* Lotion?
(MATT declines.)
Oh, that's right. You gave all this up, didn't you? Just left it all behind to "follow" him. Well, you know what they say about choice—making the wrong one stinks.
(SAUL drinks his Starbucks coffee, then lifts it high, stating proudly what it is.)
A venti salted caramel mocha frappuccino with five pumps of frap roast, four pumps of caramel syrup, three pumps of mocha, and two pumps of toffee nut syrup, double blended with extra whipped cream. *(Drinks again.)*

JESUS: The eye is the lamp of the body. So, if your eye is sound, your whole body will be full of light, but if your eye is not sound, your whole body will be full of darkness. If then the light in you is darkness, how great is the darkness!

GEORGE: *(Rises.)* But what if all you know is darkness?

MATT: He's using metaphors.

ANNA: Mata-what?!

MATT: Shhh.

JESUS: Therefore I tell you, do not be anxious about your life, what you shall eat or what you shall drink...

> *(MATT glances at SAUL, and SAUL raises a toast, then drinks.)*

JESUS: ...nor about your body, what you shall put on.

ECHO: *(Enters from the back of the house.)* Echo, here— fully certified and licensed for hire. Sorry I'm late —foot traffic. It was horrible. Just horrible. Elbow to elbow people. Everywhere.

> *(To audience.)*

My deepest, most sincere apologies to each and every one of you.

> *(ECHO begins to warm up, vocally, for echoing.)*

"Mi, mi, mi, mi, mi. Ma, ma, ma, ma, ma."

> *(Then, he quickly does some actor warm-ups, stretching his legs and shaking out his body.)*

Tickety, tackety. Tickety, tackety. Tickety—

JESUS: Is not life more than food, and the body more than clothing? Look at the birds of the air: they neither sow nor reap nor gather into barns and yet your heavenly father feeds them. Are you not of more value than they?

> *(EVERYONE on stage continues to listen to JESUS as if he is continuing to talk. They do not listen or react to ECHO as he makes his way through the audience.)*

ECHO: Maybe some of you have never had the privilege of working with a professional "Echo" before. My job, you see, is to stand in auditoriums and courtyards and hillsides like this and listen. I listen to what's being said, and then I turn around and echo it for those who are just out of earshot.
(Beat.)
When I was a mere lad, my mother called my brother and me "Pete and Repeat." "Pete and Repeat," get it? And now I do it for a living. The big time. But don't call me a "repeater;" I hate that. I'm an Echo. Echo's the name.

JESUS: But seek first his kingdom and his righteousness, and all these things shall be yours as well.

ECHO: I had this gig a few days ago for Caesar. You know, the Emperor of Rome? "Do as I say, not as I do." What a blowhard. Anyway, I finish up, get paid, and start on my way here, walking on "The Great Road." But let me tell you, there's nothing *great* about it. Then, just my luck, I stumble into this huge harem-like parade making its way North of the Sea of Galilee, so I thought, "Heck, I'll hitch a ride with them." Camels. If you don't get seasick rocking back and forth or die from saddle soars so deep they'll make your eyes water, riding camels can really save on your pads.
(Rubbing his feet.)
Well, this harem ends up being a bunch of dingbat roadies out looking for the Son of God. "The Son of God?!" Do you believe it? I mean, it's

like the Old Testament and all—those ancient predictions finally coming true—"THE MESSIAH ARRIVES!" What a joke. I wanted to cackle up a good one, but I didn't want to lose my ride—you know—the pads. *(Shaking his head.)* The Messiah coming in our lifetime. Thinking that something like that's gonna happen to us is just plain narcissism. Plain and unadulterated narcissism.

(Quickly to MATT.)

They're still going to pay me, right? I mean, if I start late, like now, will they still pay me?

MATT: I don't know.

JESUS: Do not be anxious about tomorrow, for tomorrow will be anxious for itself. Let the day's own trouble be sufficient for the day.

ECHO: If you only knew how broke I was. I haven't eaten in three days. And these ol' rags are about to fall right off my weary bones.

MATT: Yes, I can see that.

ECHO: Is that water you got there?

MATT: Yes.

ECHO: D'ya mind?

MATT: Not at all.

(MATT hands ECHO the water. ECHO drinks all of it.)

ECHO: Are you in charge?

MATT: Why don't you go see Judas? He has the purse.

ECHO: Where's he?

MATT: *(Pointing beyond audience.)* Up there, with the others.

SAUL: Up there, with the "important" people.

(ECHO looks out over the audience.)

MATT: He's the one with the furrowed brow.

ECHO: Ah! I see him. Thanks.

(Turns to go.)

Hey, what's up with the guy all "ashine?"

MATT: He's the one who's speaking. You might want to try not to distract too much. Keep your head low.

ECHO: Well, of course. Who do you think you're dealing with, anyway? I make a living at this, you know— being discreet.

(ECHO exits through audience.)

GEORGE: *(To MATT.)* How'd you do on that last segment?

MATT: *(Taking a deep breath.)* Just call me "Matthew the Paraphraser."

SAOL: *(Holding a silver sun reflector under his chin.)* That will look spectacular on your resume.

MATT: I thought you left.

SAUL: I never, *really* leave, Matt. You should know that.

MATT: What a shame. And I bet you're great with exit lines.

JESUS: Judge not, that you be not judged.

SAUL: *(To MATT.)* "Judge not, that you be not judged."

JESUS: For with the judgment you pronounce you will be judged, and the measure you give will be the measure you get.

(SAUL looks at MATT, then sees if he got all that written down.)

SAUL: Listen up, Matt.

MATT: Matthew.

(SAUL mimes the following.)

JESUS: Why do you see the speck that is in your brother's eye, but do not notice the log that is in your own eye?

MATT: Log, Matt. In your own. Eye.

JESUS: Or how can you say to your brother, 'Let me take the speck out of your eye...

SAUL: Speck. My eye. Little speck.

JESUS: ...when there is a log in your own eye? You hypocrite!

SAUL: *(To MATT.)* He said it. Not me.

(SAUL mimes taking the log out of MATT'S eye.)

JESUS: First take the log out of your own eye...

SAUL: Log...

JESUS: ...and then you will see clearly to take the speck out of your brother's eye.

SAUL: Speck!

MATT: *(To SAUL, losing his patience.)*

Why are you here? Could you please tell me that? You are nothing but a pest to us all. Here we are, trying to listen, and you do nothing but distract, irritate, and make noise. Are you aware of what's going on here today? Are you even a tad bit aware of the magnitude of this occasion? This...

(Looks at his notes because he can't remember.)

GEORGE: *(Leaning in to help.)* "Sermon on the Mountainside."

MATT: "...Sermon on the Mountainside," yes, thank you.

(Continuing to SAUL.)

This will go down in the annals as the most important words ever spoken throughout all of time. And we are here for it.

GEORGE: And you wrote it down.

MATT: I tried.

SAUL: Yes, he sure did. "Matt the Paraphraser" caught it all on cowhide folks with his new silly apparatus! Matt and his crazy writing machine—famous!!!! Is that what you want, Matt? Fame?

JESUS: Do not give dogs what is holy, and do not throw your pearls before swine, lest they trample them underfoot and turn to attack you.

ECHO: *(Re-enters, running.)* Yahoooo!!!

MATT: What in the world?

ECHO: The furrowed brow guy.

MATT: Judas?

ECHO: He's paying me. *(Beat.)* Can he be trusted?

MATT: Of course. Why do you ask?

ECHO: He says he's paying me when it's over. *(Beat.)* When is it going to be over?

MATT: I have no idea.

ECHO: No more locusts for me!

SARAH: Gross. I'd die before I'd eat locusts.

SAUL: *(To ECHO.)* You know, some people fast on purpose. Like Matt, here.

ANNA: You're fasting?!

SARAH: He just said you shouldn't boast about it, Matthew.

ANNA: How can you write all that on an empty stomach?

MATT: Please, everyone. I'm fine. Leave me alone.

ECHO: *(He does one last stretch.)*

I'm now officially in work mode.

JESUS: Ask, and it will be given you. Seek, and you will find...

ECHO: *(Striking his working pose, he begins to "echo," loudly and exaggerated, like an overacting actor.)*
"Ask, and it will be given to you; seek, and you will find."

MATT: *(To self.)* Oh, dear God.

JESUS: ...knock, and it will be opened to you.

ECHO: "Knock, and it will be opened to you."

MATT: *(To self.)* I should have sat up front. Why didn't I sit up front...with the sane?

SARAH: You said Luke was sitting up there.

MATT: What was I thinking?

JESUS: For everyone who asks receives, and he who seeks finds, and to him who knocks, it will be opened.

ECHO: "For everyone who asks receives, and he who seeks finds, and—"

MATT: *(Rises and puts his arm around ECHO.)* Listen, we appreciate your services, and I will make certain you get paid—

ECHO: *(Echoing what MATT says to the crowd.)*
"Listen, we appreciate your services, and I will make certain—
(MATT puts his hand over ECHO'S mouth.)

MATT: Could you please just repeat...

ECHO: *(Putting up a finger, correcting MATT.)* Echo.

MATT: Echo.

ECHO: *(Echoing MATT to the crowd.)* "Echo."

MATT: *(Putting his hand over ECHO'S mouth again.)*
    Could you please just echo for these two women
    here? This blind man has been...

GEORGE: *(Jumping in with his name.)* George.

MATT: George.

GEORGE: Yes.
    (Shakes MATT'S hand.)

MATT: George has been filling in for you and repeating...
    (Correcting himself.)
    Echoing, just for these two women here, and
    that's all we need.

ECHO: Fine.

SAUL: *(Sing-songy, like a limerick.)* Matt, Matt, the
    diplomat.

MATT: *(To ECHO.)* Just for them.

ECHO: Great. No problem.

MATT: Excellent.

ECHO: *(Pretending to Echo.)* "Excellent." *(Beat.)*
    Just kidding.
    *(ECHO sits by two women and repeats what
    JESUS says for them quietly. MATT returns to
    his writing.)*

JESUS: Or what man of you, if his son asks him for
    bread, will give him a stone? Or if he asks for a
    fish, will give him a serpent?

SAUL: Or if he asks for a writing machine, will give him
    an empty twig.

JESUS: If you then, who are evil, know how to give good
    gifts to your children, how much more will your
    Father who is in heaven give good things to those
    who ask him! So whatever you wish that men

would do to you, do so to them, for this is the law and the prophets.

SAUL: It's the law and the prophets, Matt.

MATT: *(Writing.)* Matthew.

SAUL: It's the law and the prophets, *Matt*, that you should give good gifts to your children.

MATT: You're not my child.

SAUL: *(Becoming an irritating child.)*

Oh, Matt. Come on, Matt. Give me the twig. Pleeeease. Pretty-pleeeease—

MATT: Matthew! Matthew! My name is Matthew. Can't you get that through your thick skull?!

JESUS: Enter by the narrow gate; for the gate is wide and the way is easy, that leads to destruction, and those who enter by it are many. For the gate is narrow and the way is hard, that leads to life, and those who find it are few.

SAUL: Matt, Matt, the little brat.

MATT: Aren't you listening at all? Even to just this—"the narrow gate?" If you could just listen to one of these beautiful concepts put forth for you by this our Messiah, one idea of his, listen, and then do it, become it, take action—just one of them, you would be changed forever.

SAUL: Changed? Whatever gave you the idea that I wanted to be changed, Matt? I don't want to be changed. It's you who wants me to change. I like me just the way I am.

JESUS: Beware of false prophets, who come to you in sheep's clothing but inwardly are ravenous wolves.

SAUL: I don't know why you don't like me, Matt.
(*Referring to what JESUS just said.*)
You see, I am a wolf, and I dress like a wolf. If
you can see me coming, how can I hurt you?

MATT: You are no wolf. I know who you are. You're a
lion looking for someone to devour.
(*SAUL gives a look. JESUS has crossed half-way
through the audience toward the group on
stage. GEORGE, SARAH, ANNA, and ECHO
have moved downstage. They begin to interact
more directly with JESUS. MATT and SAUL are
upstage of them now.*)

JESUS: You will know them by their fruits. Are grapes
gathered from thorns or figs from thistles?

EVERYONE: (*Improvising, to JESUS.*) No. No, they're
not.

JESUS: So, every sound tree bears good fruit, but the
bad tree bears evil fruit. A sound tree cannot
bear evil fruit, nor can a bad tree bear good fruit.

GEORGE: (*Shouting to JESUS.*) So what do you do with
the evil trees, Jesus?

ANNA: What do you do with evil?

JESUS: (*Answering him.*) Every tree that does not bear
good fruit is cut down and thrown into the fire.

SARAH: Lord, Lord!

SAUL: (*Taking note of the change in the group
dynamic.*)
You watch. A riot will break out here yet, and I
love riots. Live for them, actually. Try to start
them when I can.

JESUS: And not everyone who says to me, 'Lord, Lord,' shall enter the kingdom of heaven, but he who does the will of my Father who is in heaven. On that day, many will say to me, 'Lord, Lord, did we not prophesy in your name, cast out demons in your name, and do many mighty works in your name?' And then will I declare to them, 'I never knew you; depart from me, you evildoers.'

SAUL: Nice guy.

MATT: His words speak of great love.

SAUL: *(To MATT.)* This is the guy you follow around like a donkey follows a basket of grain?

MATT: If you mean he feeds my soul, then yes. I follow him like a donkey.

SAUL: *(Imitating a donkey.)* Hee, haw. Hee, haw. Crunch, crunch, crunch. Crunch, crunch, crunch.

ANNA: Lord, I am deaf. Heal me. Oh Lord, heal me. I cannot hear.

(JESUS enters the stage, through the audience, and approaches the woman in a simple manner.)

JESUS: It shall be done to you according to your faith.

ANNA: *(Suddenly, ANNA can hear.)* What? What did you say?

SARAH: He said it would be done to you according—

ANNA: Oh, thank you, Lord. Thank you.

(Falling at his feet.)

Not that I minded too much being deaf, mind you. There's really not much worth hearing these days, but how could I go on not hearing *your* beautiful words? Thank you, my Lord.

JESUS: Everyone then who hears these words of mine and does them will be like a wise man who built his house upon the rock, and then the rain fell, and the floods came, and the winds blew and beat upon that house, but it did not fall, because it had been founded on the rock.

ANNA: You alone are my rock, Lord.

JESUS: And everyone who hears these words of mine and does not do them will be like a foolish man who built his house upon the sand, and the rain fell, and the floods came, and the winds blew and beat against that house, and it fell; and great was the fall of it.

(LUKE suddenly runs through the audience and onto the stage, past MATT, and carrying his papers.)

MATT: *(Stopping LUKE as he runs by.)*
Wait. Luke, what are you doing?

LUKE: I gotta go.
(Turning to go.)

MATT: What do you mean, you gotta go. He's not finished.

LUKE: Well, he's almost done, and I want to beat foot traffic.

MATT: "Beat foot traffic?!" You can't do that! He is not done talking.

LUKE: What do you care what I do?
(Turns to go.)

MATT: This isn't about me. It's not about you. This is Jesus of Nazareth. Israel's long-awaited Messiah.

LUKE: *(Correcting him.)* He's the Son of Man.

MATT: The Messiah. We're here to document what he says for posterity.

SAUL: *(Pulling out dictionary.)* Checking my ol' trusty dictionary. Let's see...posterity. "For all succeeding generations." You go, Matt.

MATT: *(To LUKE.)* We're not writing this for ourselves. This must be a selfless thing. *(Beat.)* Let me see what you've got. Give it to me.

LUKE: No. I've got to go.

MATT: Give it here.

> *(MATT pulls LUKE'S papers from him and reads.)*
>
> "But the one who has heard and has not acted accordingly is like a man who built a house on the ground without any foundation, and the torrent burst against it, and immediately it collapsed, and the ruin of that house was great."
>
> *(Looking up at LUKE.)*
>
> "Torrent burst against it?" "Torrent?!" He didn't say "Torrent."

LUKE: Yes, he did.

MATT: No, he did not. He did not say "Torrent." He said...

> *(Looking it up in his own papers.)*
>
> "The rains fell, and the floods came, and the winds blew." That's what he said. He did not say "torrent."

LUKE: What is it you have against me, Matthew? What did I ever do to you? Is it the interview I got with Mary? Is that what's bothering you?

MATT: It's not about you. Don't you see? It's about your writing. You never get it right.

LUKE: I'm not trying to get it perfectly right. I'm trying to get it written.

MATT: Well, that's not good enough!

LUKE: Give it to me. I've got to go.

MATT: No.

LUKE: Give it to me, Matthew.

MATT: I'll give it to you when you deserve to write about the Son of God.

(Suddenly, LUKE jumps on top of MATT and tries to get his pages back.)

MATT: *(Continuing.)* What are you doing?! Get off me, Luke!

LUKE: You're just a jealous little Jew! You know that.

MATT: Gentiles can't write the word of God. You've proven that with your sophisticated Greek.

LUKE: Well, Gentiles are going to read it too! It's for everyone, Matthew. Not just you Jews!

(THEY are fighting and rolling around on the ground. JESUS crosses to them and watches.)

LUKE: Give it to me!

MATT: No.

LUKE: I said give it to me.

MATT: I said no.

JESUS: *(Standing above them.)* Matthew.

(THEY recognize his voice and stop.)

MATT: Yes, my Lord.

JESUS: Variety is one of my Father's attributes. There are many followers and many ways to pierce their guarded hearts.

MATT: Yes, my Lord.

LUKE: Thank you, Jesus.

> *(LUKE kisses JESUS' feet and runs off.)*

SAUL: *(To MATT.)* "Yes, my Lord. Yes, my Lord." What a mealworm you are, Matt. Isn't there anything you can say but "Yes, my Lord?"

JESUS: And as for you...

SAUL: *(Mocking MATT.)* "Yes, my Lord?"

MATT: He's not worth your time. He's riddled with demons.

SAUL: Demons? I don't have any demons. This is just my natural, vibrant personality. I've been like this forever.

JESUS: What are you afraid of?

SAUL: Me, "afraid?" Why, I've never been afraid of anything in my—

> *(JESUS crosses to SAUL and places his hands on his heart.)*

SAUL: Life.

> *(SAUL is deeply moved and begins to actually weep. All of his pretentious behavior dissolves before us because of the love penetrating into him through Jesus' hand.)*

> Oh, my Lord. Please forgive me.

> *(Drops to his knees.)*

> Forgive me.

MATT: Oh. My God.

> *(MATT is amazed by this, grabs his paper and writing apparatus, and begins to write it all down.)*

JESUS: Go, and sin no more.

SAUL: Yes, my Lord.

> *(He rises and looks at his pile of things. Sheepishly.)*

Can I take my things with me, or do I have to leave them all behind now? 'Cause I use this chair a lot, and this sunscreen has been very beneficial. My skin is so susceptible to the damaging effects of the sun. And let's not even mention my Starbucks addiction... Quite honestly, I don't know what I'd do without my Starbucks.

MATT: *(Picking up SAUL'S stuff and handing it to him.)* Just take it. Take it all, and don't bug anyone anymore.

SAUL: Thank you, Matt—Matthew. I'm grateful. It's Matthew, right? Yes, I'm sure it is. I appreciate you. "So long, farewell, auf Wiedersehen, goodbye."

> *(SAUL exits with all his stuff.)*

MATT: I knew he'd be good with exit lines.

SARAH: *(Crosses to JESUS.)* Excuse me? Sir?

> *(JESUS turns to SARAH.)*

SARAH: I was wondering what I should do with my life now that I cannot remarry. I mean, anyone who marries me now will be committing adultery.

JESUS: Take courage, woman. Your sins are forgiven.

SARAH: But what if it wasn't me who sinned?

> *(MATT continues to document all of what is said.)*

JESUS: If you judge poetry because a poet deceived you—

SARAH: How did you know?

JESUS: ...then you are not free because you judge falsely and do not live in truth, and therefore, you sin.

MATT: *(To SARAH.)* Did you get that?

SARAH: I think so. But it might help me to go over it from time to time.

MATT: *(Tearing the page from his book.)* Here, it's yours. Take it with you.

SARAH: Really? Thank you, Matthew. That writing instrument of yours sure has turned out to be a gift from God. Thank you so very much.
(SARAH goes to kiss MATT.)

MATT: Oh, no. Give him the glory.

SARAH: Yes, of course.
(SARAH kisses JESUS on the side of his face.)

SARAH: *(To MATT.)* Bye there.
(A little wave.)

MATT: Bye, there.
(A wave.)

ECHO: *(Crosses to MATT.)* Hey, thanks, man.
(Shakes his coins in his little sack.)
Got my dough, heading to my next gig. Sorry again for being late.

MATT: It all worked out. It always does. I don't know why I worry.

ECHO: *(Shakes his coins again, suddenly spots JESUS.)* Hey! There he is—the star of the show! Dude, I gotta tell ya, nice speech. You really hit it out of the park, and I should know. I've heard 'em all. You wouldn't believe the useless information I echo, day in and day out, but this stuff was ground-breaking, mind-blowing, riv-et-ting!!!

You are an inspiration. You nearly had *me*
believing it.

JESUS: This is the work of God, that you believe in Him
whom He has sent.

ECHO: When I get everything I need together, and my
ducks are in a row, I will make the time for all
this "Love God, love each other stuff." But for
now, "Gotta gig; gotta go."

(He shakes the coins and begins to exit.)

JESUS: Seek first the kingdom of God, and His
righteousness; and all these things shall be added
unto you.

(ECHO is gone.)

MATT: Good riddance.

JESUS: Matthew, you look anxious. How can I remove
your worries?

MATT: By removing idiots like that. What's their
problem, anyway?

JESUS: They don't believe the Messiah has arrived
because there's still evil in the world. But
lawlessness will increase, and people will stop
showing their love for each other. But those who
keep their faith until the end will be saved.

MATT: If I were you, I would just force them to believe.

JESUS: And take away their choice?

MATT: *(Agreeing, with discouragement)* I guess you're
right.

JESUS: Are these your pages?

MATT: Yeah. Well, they're *your* pages.

JESUS: *(Reading from them.)* "Therefore do not be
anxious about tomorrow, for tomorrow will be

anxious for itself. Let the day's own trouble be sufficient for the day." *(Beat.)* Did you write this?

MATT: Yes.

JESUS: Until we are with my Father who is in heaven, the test of the prophet is the prophet's life. What worries you the most?

MATT: You leaving us one day, and I didn't get it all written.

JESUS: I will ask the Father, and he will send you a helper—the Holy Spirit. You will know him because he will abide with you and be in you.

MATT: *(Confused.)* So, you're saying I can write about your life, here on earth, and everything you said *after* you've gone?

(JESUS nods, and MATT is in disbelief.)

JESUS: Your goosebumps. Trust your goosebumps.

MATT: *(MATT smiles and understands.)* Ah, yes. I understand. I will, Jesus. I will trust you.

JESUS: What's this?

MATT: Oh, it's a writing apparatus I put together.

JESUS: How did it work for you?

MATT: Well, you know us humans. We may change, but we don't change much.

JESUS: Yes.

MATT: Here I had the gadget, the apparatus I thought would solve all my problem, and it was you all along. I just needed to spend a moment or two with you.

JESUS: Nice.

MATT: *(Suddenly serious.)* I know you gotta go someday, but don't go yet, Jesus. Please.

JESUS: No. Not yet. Keep writing, Matthew. It suits you.

MATT: *(Smiles and nods.)* I will.

JESUS: The foxes have holes, and the birds of the air have nests, but the Son of Man has nowhere to lay his head. I'm tired. *(Beat.)* Matthew, will you come with me?

MATT: I will follow you wherever you go.

(MATT and JESUS begin to exit.)

GEORGE: *(Humbly, clearing his throat.)* Uhmm. Excuse me? Messiah?

(MATT and JESUS turn back.)

I don't mean to hold you up or anything, but... Well, I'm just a man—an old man, at that. But I was wondering—

JESUS: Your Father in Heaven knows what you need before you ask.

GEORGE: *(He senses something, then reaches up to his eyes.)*

Oh, my Lord! Look. Matthew, look. Everyone, I can see. Look at me. I can see.

JESUS: Go and tell no one.

MATT: *(Sarcastically referring to GEORGE.)*

What are the chances of that?

GEORGE: *(As he runs offstage, we hear him all the way.)*

Hey, look, everyone! I can see. This man, this Jesus, he didn't even have to touch me, and I've been healed. I can see!

MATT: They can never keep a secret, can they?

JESUS: Oh, a lot of them do. You just never hear those stories.

GEORGE: Look! Look! Everyone! I can seeee. I can seeeeeeeeeee...

(He runs out as the lights fade out.)

END OF PLAY

PERSONAL PROPERTIES

SAUL: a dictionary, band-aids, a lawn chair, a small table, suntan lotion, a sun hat, a silver sun reflector, a sack lunch, and a large Starbucks coffee.

MATTHEW: a scroll, a writing apparatus made of wood, a jar of ink, and a leather water skin filled with water.

COSTUMES

Eight, first-century tunics, some have head dressings, belts, and/or purses.

LISA SOLAND'S PLAYS

AN AFTERNOON WITH SHIRLEY and THE EMPTY
     CHAIR: Complementary One-Act Plays
CABO SAN LUCAS (Samuel French & Smith and Kraus)
THE CHRISTMAS TREE ANGEL RADIO DRAMA
COME TO THE GARDEN (Samuel French)
THE CORPORATE LADDER (Smith and Kraus)
DIFFERENT (Samuel French & Smith and Kraus)
DR. BISCOTTI & THE HUMAN CONDITION (All
     Original Play Publishing)
AN EARTHQUAKE (Dramatic Publishing)
THE FREEWHEELIN' BOB DYLAN (Quay Magazine)
THE HAND ON THE PLOUGH
HAPPY BIRTHDAY, BABY!
HOORAY FOR HOLLYWOOD (All Original Play
     Publishing)
IN THE UPPER ROOM (All Original Play Publishing)
INSPIRED! A Drama With Music
THE KIND THAT DOESN'T BUDGE (Samuel French &
     Quay Magazine)
KNOTS (Samuel French & Smith and Kraus)
THE LADDER IN THE ROOM (Applause Books)
THE LADDER PLAYS
THE MAN IN THE GRAY SUIT (Samuel French)
MATT & HIS CRAZY WRITING MACHINE (All Original
     Play Publishing)
MEET CUTE
THE NAME GAME (Samuel French)
THE OTHER SHOE (Smith and Kraus)
THE ReBIRTH (Applause Books)
REBOUND AND THE BATHTUB
RED ROSES (Samuel French & Applause Books)
THE SAME THING (Samuel French & Smith and Kraus)
SERGEANT YORK: THE PLAY (All Original Play
     Publishing)
SENSITIVITY (Samuel French)
THE SNIPER'S NEST
SPATIAL DISORIENTATION (Applause Books)
THREAD COUNT (Applause Books)
TRUTH BE TOLD (Samuel French & Quay Magazine)
WAITING (Samuel French, Smith and Kraus, & Applause
Books)

What they're saying about
30 SHORT PLAYS
FOR PASSIONATE ACTORS...

"Lisa Soland has here assembled a wonderful collection of short plays. If you're a passionate actor, a teacher or a director looking for a play to do, you won't find a better place to start looking than this book."
— *Lawrence Harbison, Senior Editor, Smith and Kraus & Applause Theatre & Cinema Books*

"Lisa Soland's amazing collection of 30 excellent, sooo entertaining short plays is a must for any would-be playwright, actor or acting group!"
— *Tom Sawyer, novelist, playwright, screenwriter*

"This collection of plays is as varied and eclectic as the human mind itself. They are funny, dramatic, poignant, shocking, outrageous, satirical, imaginative... It's a must-have for writers of short plays and a great resource for theatres that produce them."
— *Peter Colley, playwright, screenwriter, librettist*

What they're saying about
SERGEANT YORK: THE PLAY

"It's simply a wonderful play."
– Deborah York, Executive Director of the Sergeant York Patriotic Foundation and great-granddaughter of Alvin York

"Sergeant York: The Play is... a powerful statement on the nature of war and the power of faith."
– Peter Colley, playwright/screenwriter/librettist

"I thoroughly recommend *Sergeant York: The Play* for any organization seeking an inspirational, wholesome tale of a true American hero."
– Burt Rosen, President and CEO of Knox Area Rescue Ministries Knoxville

"Soland has devoted her significant abilities to share the story of Alvin York's deep personal faith and commitment to Jesus Christ."
– Sam Polson, Lead Pastor of West Park Baptist Church